## About the Book

Will the island of Puerto Rico become the 51st state of the Union? Will it become an independent country? Or will it remain a commonwealth, keeping and improving its present form of government, which is unique in all the world?

This book reviews these questions for young Stateside Americans, through the eyes of a Puerto Rican family of nine with whom readers visit the island.

In the course of the visit they learn how Puerto Rico, once a Spanish possession, came to be American, and how the people of the island combine Spanish, African and American ways of life. The island tour includes some of the worst slums in the world and some of the brightest new housing projects. How the people of Puerto Rico are lifting themselves from poverty to a decent life, and in so doing setting an example for other developing countries of the world is an important theme of this story.

The Ramírez family, whom readers of this book get to know, is on the way up. The family has relatives among the one million Puerto Ricans in the mainland United States, and some day the Ramírezes want to visit them — but not to stay. Since the 1940's and 50's when Puerto Ricans fled to the mainland from the poverty of their islands, the tide has turned. Today many Stateside Puerto Ricans are returning home.

By getting to know the Ramírez family, it's easy to discover the attraction of the island. On vacation, the family squeezes into a small car and takes off for village festivals where people dance in the streets to honor patron saints. En route, the road climbs high in the mountains through a rain forest, verdant and moist as a giant greenhouse. Indian caves, coffee and sugarcane plantations, pineapple fields, a glittering phosphorescent bay, tobacco farms, and narrow-alleyed old San Juan, the island's capital, are all part of the vacation tour.

## About the Illustrator

HARIS PETIE, who studied under Norman Rockwell in Paris, is equally at home with nations and children. Mother of two, this widely traveled, long-time illustrator of children's books has illustrated fifteen Getting to Know books with a grace which grows from respect for readers and text.

*About the Author*

To complete field research for this book, FRANCES ROLLINS spent several weeks with the people readers meet in its pages. She traveled throughout Puerto Rico discovering first-hand how the people of this beautiful island live.

Mrs. Rollins has acted as a consultant for The Experiment in International Living, the youth division of the NAACP, the Governor's Fact Finding Commission on Education in Connecticut, and for citizens' groups working with the schools of New York, Philadelphia and Chicago. Born in Worcester, Massachusetts, she graduated from Vassar College and is the mother of two daughters whose busy careers equal her own.

*About the* Getting to Know *Series*

This round-the-world series not only covers everyday life in many countries and regions and includes their geography and history, but also highlights what's new today. The series offers timely — and often first — reports on the birth of new nations in Africa and Asia; the splitting of ancient nations, like China; the let's-get-together movements of members of Europe's and Latin America's common markets; and the struggle of two-thirds of the world to attain the good life possessed by the other third. To keep each book up-to-date in these fast-changing times, it is revised with every new printing.

Specific countries in the Getting to Know series are determined by a survey of curriculum specialists in the fifty states. Made every two years, the survey is used to relate GTK subject matter to classroom needs. To ensure intimacy, as well as immediacy, authors are chosen first of all for the quality of their personal experience with the subject matter. All Getting to Knows are also checked by experts prior to publication.

# Getting to Know
# *PUERTO RICO*

by FRANCES ROLLINS

illustrated by HARIS PETIE

COWARD-McCANN, Inc.                                    NEW YORK

The author would like to acknowledge with appreciation the guidance and information given her in the preparation of this book by Messrs. Rafael de Santiago and Maurice J. Phillips of Fomento; Mr. Andres Mignucci of CRUV; Mrs. Americo de la Cruz and Mr. Laurido Soto, directors of CRUV housing project community center for children; Mr. Nicolas Princz and Mrs. Carmen Gandára of Olympic Mills; Mr. Carlos E. Ramírez of the U. S. Forest Service; William J. Dorvillier, publisher of the San Juan *Star;* Mr. Jaime Gonzalez Carló and Mrs. Alice Jiménez de Rigau of the Puerto Rican Department of Public Education; Mr. and Mrs. Joaquim Kino Velez of San Germán; Mr. Herbert Abel of Ponce; Sis and Carl Frank, Henry, Ilsa and Richard Klumb.

For a friend of Puerto Rico and a member of its Status Commission
LEO W. O'BRIEN

*Library of Congress Catalog Card Number: AC 67-10424*

## GETTING TO KNOW PUERTO RICO

"The island of Borinquén where I was born
Is a garden of flowers of magic beauty...."

Singing together to the music of the bands, boys and girls from many schools are marching in the parade along the Avenue Ponce de León from the old to the new part of San Juan, the capital of Puerto Rico. Soldiers, firemen, policemen, with flower-decked floats in between, are also marching to the music.

It is July 25. On that date, since 1952, the people of Puerto Rico have been celebrating Commonwealth Day. That is the date when the Commonwealth, Puerto Rico's democratic form of local government, was founded.

The people sing mostly in Spanish, the language of Puerto Rico. But they are proud that their Commonwealth is part of the United States, proud that they are American citizens.

So, on this July 25th, all along the avenue and shaded from the beating sun by broad-leafed almond trees, parents and children, uncles and aunts, grandfathers and grandmothers stand for three hours to watch the parade. Many of the children wave little Puerto Rican flags — a white star in a blue triangle against red and white horizontal stripes. Some children wave both Puerto Rican and American flags.

The island of Puerto Rico lies between North and South America a little more than halfway between the tip of Florida and the northern coast of Venezuela. It is a sort of gatepost between the Atlantic Ocean and the Caribbean Sea. The island is small — a little smaller than Connecticut — but it is important to North America. This is because the island is making such a success of solving its problem of too many people, not enough land.

Puerto Rico has two and a half million people — more people for its size than almost any other place in the world. It is ten times as thickly settled as the United States. All the people in the world, except those in India and Pakistan, would have to move to the U.S.A. to make it as densely populated as Puerto Rico. In the countryside, as well as in the towns and cities, the island is too crowded. This has always been a big problem.

In 1940 most Puerto Ricans were horribly poor. People who visited Puerto Rico at that time saw misery, disease, and dirt everywhere. Most farm workers, or *jíbaros,* as they are called in Spanish, earned about $135 a year — less than 40¢ a day. A father with a family of five did well if he earned $600 a year, hardly enough to feed his family. Today the same man may earn $4,500 or more a year, enough so that he and his family can live well. Yet today many people in neighboring countries in South America and the Caribbean Sea are still as poor as Puerto Rico was in 1940. These people want to follow Puerto Rico's example.

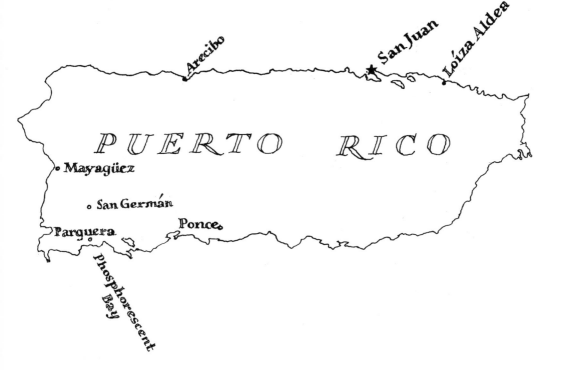

ATLANTIC OCEAN

Arecibo

San Juan

Lóiza Aldea

PUERTO RICO

Mayagüez

San Germán

Ponce

Parguera

Phosphorescent Bay

CARIBBEAN SEA

The Puerto Ricans have learned from experience that they have not enough land for everyone to make a good living by farming. Now they are learning that if you can't grow *out,* you can grow *up.* They are building new schools, new houses, new hospitals, and new factories.

The island's growth is the reason why several thousand visitors from other developing countries come to Puerto Rico every year. Some of them come from South and Central America and the other Caribbean islands. Others come from far away, from the many new and struggling nations of Asia and Africa. All of them come to learn the secrets of the island's success.

The visitors find it exciting to see the improvements. But what the visitors see today is far from what the Puerto Ricans want to have for themselves before long. Children and grown-ups are busily working. They are making — and putting into action — plans for getting many more things done as fast as they can. More and more people are moving up to better jobs. This means that they are able to move into better houses and live more comfortably. But these lucky people cannot forget their friends and relatives who are still poor and miserable.

In the cities, a third of Puerto Rico's people live in slums which have been called the worst in the world. Many jíbaros live in shanties no better than the city slums except that in the country there is fresh air to breathe. Whether he is in the city or the country, one worker out of every nine still has no job.

So there is still much to be done in Puerto Rico. Nobody knows it better than the people who are parading in the streets on Commonwealth Day. They are working together, as they are marching together — both grown-ups and children — to make a brighter future for all.

You feel this as you stand there, watching the parade. Look! Here come the huge yellow Caterpillar earthmovers. The enormous machines are growling and belching diesel smoke as the drivers twist and turn the dump shovels left and right toward the spectators. Construction workmen march behind the earthmover machines. The men are wearing bright orange helmets. It takes know-how to operate these machines, and know-how means education.

In 1940, three out of every ten Puerto Ricans couldn't read. Today, only one in ten can't. But still there aren't enough schools and enough teachers. The Commonwealth spends a little more than a third of its budget on education. The money is used to build more schools, train more teachers, send more children through high school and college, and educate their parents.

The schools are well represented in the parade. Teachers march with their students. Then come the bookmobiles — bus-libraries that travel to villages high in the hills and through the sugarcane fields in the valleys. The schoolchildren, the girls dressed in white, the boys in white shirts and blue trousers, carry banners with the names of their schools, or of the school clubs to which they belong. Here come the English Clubs, their banners bearing the slogan MORE AND BETTER ENGLISH.

Following the school clubs come other groups to which children belong: the Police Athletic League, 4-H members, and on their bikes you see Boy Scouts in khaki and Girl Scouts in green uniforms. Next are the Junior Firemen, both girls and boys, waving and shouting from the fire truck, the *camión de bomberos,* into which they are packed. The Junior Firemen wear scarlet helmets, scarlet shirts and blue jeans. A helicopter is circling overhead as, group by group, the long parade of men, women and children from all over Puerto Rico files past the Capitol.

The Capitol is a striking symbol of today's Puerto Rico. The building is a mixture of very old and very modern. The style of

the central part comes from ancient Greece. It is made of marble. Curly-topped Corinthian pillars guard the main entrance, and simple Ionic columns line the wings. But on either side of the building, there is a pair of modern annexes of glistening glass, concrete and chrome. These recent additions to the building say plainly, "The time is today."

Inside the Capitol, Puerto Rico's Legislative Assembly meets. The Assembly's Senate and House of Representatives are elected by the people. The people also elect their own Chief Executive, the Governor.

Puerto Ricans must obey the laws passed by their own legislature, and like other American citizens, they must also obey the laws passed by the United States Congress. For instance, they are subject to our draft law. Puerto Ricans serve in the American Army side by side with other U. S. citizens, and the United States is responsible for defending Puerto Rico in case of war.

In Washington, a Resident Commissioner from Puerto Rico advises Congress on laws which affect the island. When they move to the U. S. mainland where they come under local laws, Puerto Ricans, like other Americans, cast their votes for the President of the United States. At home in Puerto Rico, they vote only for their own local officials. There is a special system of taxes which pays for the cost of government services to the people. Puerto Ricans pay only local income taxes. However, they pay certain other United States taxes for services which affect them directly — such as Social Security which helps take care of people when they are old or sick.

Like the fifty states of the Union, Puerto Rico receives money from the U. S. Treasury to assist in building houses, running schools and paying for other basic needs. Much of the money which comes to Puerto Rico from the U. S. Treasury results from the association between the U. S. A. and the island. For example, if your father buys a bottle of Puerto Rican rum in the United States, he pays a tax on it. The Treasury pays Puerto Rico this "rum money" — the tax income from rum making, which is big business in Puerto Rico.

So you can see how the commonwealth form of government divides power and money between the United States and Puerto Rico. It is unlike any other form of government in the world. To find out how it developed, we must know something about Puerto Rican, Spanish and American History.

Columbus discovered the island on his second voyage to the Western Hemisphere and claimed it for Spain. He found the Arawak Indians living there. Their name for the island was "Borinquén," a name kept alive by the children in the parade as they march along singing in Spanish their favorite anthem. In Spanish, it is called "La Borinqueña." The English translation says:

> "The island of Borinquén where I was born,
> Is a garden of flowers of magic beauty.
> A sky always clear
> Serves as its canopy.
> And the placid ocean
> Murmurs around it.
> On the day long ago,
> When Columbus arrived in its harbor,
> He exclaimed full of admiration,
> 'Oh! Oh! Oh!
> This is the beautiful island
> For which I have been seeking.
> Borinquén is the island
> The island of sun and sea —
> Of sun and sea!' "

For some reason of his own, Columbus did not use the Indian name "Borinquén." He called the island "San Juan Bautista"; in

STATUE
OF PONCE de LEÓN

English, "St. John the Baptist." One of the men in his crew was Ponce de León, who later became Puerto Rico's first governor. Still later Ponce de León journeyed north in search of the "fountain of youth" and discovered Florida.

Puerto Rico was an important discovery for the Spanish because of its fine harbor. This was the port the Spanish used to ship back to Spain the gold they found in Mexico. That is why they called the town which grew up around the port "Puerto Rico, "rich port." It was not until later that the whole island was called Puerto Rico and the harbor town was called San Juan.

Spanish rule of Puerto Rico was hard on everybody: the Arawaks, the Negroes whom the Spanish brought from Africa as slaves, and the Spanish themselves. The Arawaks, who had led carefree lives, hunting, farming and fishing, were forced into hard labor. Some died from overwork. Others died of diseases which the Spanish brought from Europe. Still others died fighting against their masters. The few who survived fled to neighboring islands.

By 1511, eighteen years after Columbus discovered the island, the Spanish were growing coffee, tobacco and sugarcane on big plantations. They made their Negro slaves work so hard that, like the Indians, many of them died and many others ran away. When the slaves were not toiling in the fields, they were hauling huge blocks of stone to build forts.

16

At that time several nations in Europe were fighting for possession of lands in the Caribbean, so the Spanish rulers were constantly worried about enemy attacks. They were most in fear of the Dutch, the French, and the British. Because Puerto Rico stands at the entrance of the Caribbean Sea, the Spanish felt that they needed to make the island strong enough not only to defend itself, but also to protect their other possessions in the region. They made their forts so strong and guarded them so well that after 1797 no other country tried to invade Puerto Rico.

However, adventurers from England, France, Denmark, Portugal and Holland found another way to get a share of Puerto Rico's rich produce. They brought their ships into port at other settlements around the island where there were no forts with powerful guns to keep their ships at a distance. In these settlements, they traded slaves and cloth for long-horned cattle, pigs, fruits and other fresh foods to replenish their ships.

According to Spanish law, Puerto Ricans were not supposed to trade with any other country except Spain. But by 1815, the Spanish saw that the only way to stop the illegal smuggling was to allow Puerto Rico to trade freely with other countries. Then the island began to prosper. Coffee had replaced sugarcane as the principal crop, and this attracted merchant ships from many countries of Europe. The chance to grow moneymaking crops drew settlers from Spain, Denmark, Ireland, Portugal, France, England, and the United States.

These new settlers naturally wanted some voice in the government of their adopted country. In 1897, under the leadership of a wise and strong man, Luis Muñoz Rivera, they finally forced Spain to give it to them. Then came the Spanish American War in 1898, and suddenly, just as the Puerto Ricans won at least a beginning of self-rule, the colony changed hands.

The war lasted only a little more than three months. The Americans won, and Spain turned Puerto Rico and some of her other possessions over to the United States. For the next two years the American Army ruled the island.

The Puerto Ricans had very little chance to take part in the government that replaced the U. S. Army rule. Except for one house of the legislature, government officials were appointed by the President of the United States. Muñoz Rivera was still leading the fight for more self-rule as he had when the Spanish governed the island. The result was that in 1917, the U. S. Congress passed an act which said that Puerto Ricans were now American citizens with the right to elect both houses of their legislature.

You can see why the people of Puerto Rico think of Luis Muñoz Rivera as the father of their country. To them, he is as well known as George Washington is to you. In almost every Puerto Rican town there is a square, or school or street named for him.

Now at last the Puerto Ricans could elect their own lawmakers, even though their governor was still appointed in Washington by the President of the United States. Led by Luis Muñoz Marín, the son of Luis Muñoz Rivera, many Puerto Ricans decided to keep on trying for more self-government.

The United States was slow in giving the Puerto Rican people their political rights, but it did give attention to their physical needs. Only a very few people in Puerto Rico were rich and prosperous. The poor were very poor, and there were a great many of them. They lived in ramshackle huts, which were without sanitation. Many of them were sick and unable to make a living. More than half the children never had a chance to go to school.

The United States Public Health Service sent doctors and nurses to work with Puerto Ricans throughout the island. They helped

cure malaria and tuberculosis — diseases that were killing hundreds of people every year. They taught how to prevent these diseases. American educators set up a public school system. Other experts started programs to build new houses. Still others turned rough roads and mule trails into good truck roads. The poor people in Puerto Rico began to have an opportunity to learn how to earn more money and live a little better.

In this opportunity, young Muñoz Marín saw the path to Commonwealth. He was determined to do much more, much faster. But he knew that only healthy, hopeful, educated people could be expected to govern themselves wisely. "Let us forget about fighting for more self-government for a while," he told the people. "Let us spend all our energy pulling ourselves up by our bootstraps. When

we have done this, we shall be in a stronger position to argue about our rights." So in 1940, to put his ideas into action, he started the self-help program called Operation Bootstrap.

Operation Bootstrap meant that the poor people in Puerto Rico at last began to find new ways to make a living. Farmers learned that by using new methods of agriculture, their land yielded more.

Most Puerto Rican farmers had growing children. They tried to think of what would be best for their families in the long run. In the beginning, sometimes they had even less than before and had to work twice as hard. But the farmers knew they would win in the end. They began to use only half of what they raised on the farm for food. The other half of the grain they planted or sold in the market. This meant that every year they grew more and had more to sell.

Through Operation Bootstrap the Puerto Ricans discovered that right there at home they could make some of the things they needed. They began to build factories. What they didn't need for themselves, they found they could sell to outsiders. They learned that in this way they could earn money to pay for other things they needed.

Caonillas Dam

One Operation Bootstrap project took waterpower from the rivers as they rushed down the hills and changed it into electric power to serve factories and farms. Many people, instead of half starving on poor farms, moved into the towns to work in the new factories. Operation Bootstrap ran education projects, housing projects, and many others. All of them aimed to help Puerto Ricans live better.

American experts helped Luis Muñoz Marín get Operation Bootstrap started. One of these men was Rexford Tugwell, who was governor of Puerto Rico from September 19, 1941 to September 2, 1946. The Puerto Ricans learned to admire, and also to love him as they worked together to set up a Planning Board.

The job of the Planning Board was to find out how to divide what the island had so that it would do the most good for all Puerto Rico. Mr. Tugwell and the men on the Board showed the people how they could best use the money available to pay for things the island needed most. Under his guidance, they found out how they could have more and better bus and telephone service, airports, housing, and sewage and water supplies.

Operation Bootstrap set up special corporations to operate these public services. The corporations are controlled by the government, but they operate much like private businesses. When they show good earnings, they can borrow from banks to expand. One of the most important of these corporations — half government, half private — is called "Fomento." *Fomento* is a Spanish word meaning "stir up." The job of this corporation is to stir up business for Puerto Rico and jobs for Puerto Ricans.

Fomento has branch offices in the United States and in other interested countries. These branch offices are busy attracting manufacturers who want to build factories in Puerto Rico. The government of Puerto Rico chooses areas of the island where the most people need jobs. A business firm that agrees to set up shop in such an area doesn't have to pay taxes for up to seventeen years.

You can see signs of Fomento's success everywhere in Puerto Rico. You see familiar signs like: GRAND UNION . . . GENERAL ELECTRIC . . . WOOLWORTH . . . COCA-COLA . . . ESSO . . . KODAK . . . FORD MOTORS. You see Puerto Rico's progress in other ways, too: the growing number of television aerials which tell how many people can afford TV sets; the full parking lots by the housing projects which show how many people can buy cars; the road workers busy making new boulevards to take care of the growing traffic; and the new houses and well-stocked supermarkets in every city. Puerto Ricans thank Operation Bootstrap for these good things.

When Muñoz Marín was satisfied that Bootstrap was on its way, he decided the time had come for what he called *Operation Commonwealth*. True to his word, for several years he had spent most of his energy in getting the self-help programs started. At the same time, he had never really stopped his efforts to get the United States to give Puerto Rico more self-rule. Imagine how happy he was, in 1947, when at last the U. S. Congress agreed to let the Puerto Ricans vote for their own Governor. Furthermore, Congress gave the Governor the right to choose his own cabinet. Three years later, Congress passed a law permitting the Puerto Ricans to draw up their own Constitution, subject to Congressional approval. The new Constitution marked the beginning of the present Commonwealth.

With Bootstrap running well and the Commonwealth achieved, Muñoz Marín started "Operation Serenidad." As you might guess, *Serenidad* is Spanish for "serenity," but in this case it doesn't mean exactly that. To the Puerto Ricans it means that they know there's more to life than things like the television sets, automobiles and supermarkets resulting from *Operation Bootstrap*.

Operation Serenidad means opportunities for everyone to get more education, to make or hear music, to enjoy painting or looking at pictures, and to read or to write books. It means using part of the time once needed in the struggle simply to *make* a living — to relax and really *enjoy* living. Muñoz Marín wanted to make sure that Puerto Ricans didn't become slaves to *things*.

Probably Luis Muñoz Marín could have been reelected as governor for life, but in 1964 he refused to run again. He thought it was not democratic for one man to stay too long in office. However, the good programs he mapped out for Puerto Rico are still going on, and as you travel around the island you see them in action. Much of what you see will make you think, Yes, this is Operation Bootstrap — or Operation Commonwealth, or Operation Serenidad.

Perhaps you're lucky enough to begin to get acquainted with Puerto Rico by visiting some people you met while you were watching the Commonwealth Day parade. They invite you to go home with them for supper. Fourteen-year-old José Ramírez de Rosas and his twelve-year-old sister, Inocencia, marched with the English clubs. Their younger sisters, Salvadora, ten, and Felícita, nine, rode their bikes with the Girl Scouts. Their seven-year-old twin brothers, Flavio and Flores, and little Laly who is five, were too young to march. They were watching the parade with their parents.

When your friends introduced you to Mr. and Mrs. Ramírez de Rosas, you already knew that you should call them "Mr. and Mrs. Ramírez." The name "de Rosas" was the maiden name of Mr. Ramírez' mother. It is used when members of the family sign their full names, but it isn't used in conversation. According to Spanish custom, children carry the mother's name in this way. That's why the son of Luis Muñoz *Rivera* was named Luis Muñoz *Marín*.

The Ramírez family lives in a public housing project just outside San Juan. It's almost suppertime when you arrive with them at their apartment in the family car. Salvadora and Felícita come along soon after on their bikes. Mrs. Ramírez brings you a cool drink and asks you to make yourself at home. One by one, everybody disappears to change from holiday clothes to everyday ones. Off with the stiff, shiny shoes and on with the comfortable sandals!

This is the time of day when the whole housing project is filled with hungry-making odors. As Mrs. Ramírez goes to work at the stove, tempting smells begin to waft through the apartment. From the window you see a few chickens pecking in the yard. José points out his pet rooster, Joaquim, and assures you that he wouldn't think of eating *him;* any other chicken but not Joaquim!

Most of the neighbors who are cooking chicken are making *arroz con pollo*, José explains . . . chicken and rice. But you will have something even better, he tells you. His mother has made *paella*. This is chicken and rice to which she has added seafoods — rice, shrimp, lobster and squid. Squid is a kind of octopus — a stranger to most of us, but a familiar favorite in Puerto Rico.

Before long, Mrs. Ramírez and the girls bring to the table heaping platters of paella and fried plantain. The plantain looks something like fried banana, but it is more solid and it's not so sweet as banana. The whole family gathers around the table. A large picture of Christ, on the wall above, seems to look down on them, blessing them all. Before they sit down, Mr. Ramírez says grace — a thank-you prayer for the good food; for like most Puerto Rican families, Mr. and Mrs. Ramírez and their children are devout Roman Catholics.

There is a comfortable silence as everybody begins to eat, but the quiet doesn't last long. In a few minutes everybody wants to talk about the fun they had at the parade. Sometimes it seems to you that they're all talking at once and you don't understand when they talk so fast in Spanish. But luckily, José and Inocencia speak excellent English. They translate quickly for you. Now they are talking about their new house.

The house is partly built. Mr. Ramírez is doing most of the work

himself, with the help of some friends — the same friends he helped last year when they were building their house. He bought the roof and the supporting columns for his house from CRUV, one of Operation Bootstrap's Fomento corporations. CRUV stands for *C*orporación de *R*enovación *U*rbana y *V*ivienda. Salvadora tells you that this means "Corporation for Urban Renewal and Living."

Mr. and Mrs. Ramírez saved a long time for the house. Every month they put twenty dollars into CRUV's Housing Bank. The Bank added ten dollars to their twenty. When they had enough for a down payment, the bank loaned them the rest of the money for the house at a very low rate of interest.

Mr. Ramírez didn't have to pay for the land on which he is building the house. The Government owns it, but he and his family will always have the right to live there. If they ever sell their house, they can also sell the right to the land. Puerto Ricans call this custom "usufruct," meaning "use-fruit." It's an expression which goes back to the times when people were allowed to pick the fruit from trees they didn't own themselves. It will be easy for Mr. Ramírez to add to the house later if the family grows bigger. It probably will, for to Puerto Ricans seven children is not very many. Maybe there will be nine or ten in the family some day.

José and Inocencia are more excited about the new house than the other children. They are old enough to remember the place where they lived before they moved into the housing project. The place was called "El Fanguito." The nice way to say El Fanguito

in English is "the mudhole," but José and Inocencia tell you that most of the people who lived there called it "the sewer." The bad-smelling waste water in El Fanguito ran through open channels down a cliff to the sea. On either side of the channels were tiny pavements where people could walk. The pavements were so narrow that you had to walk by putting one foot carefully in front of the other as though you were on a tightrope. The Ramírez family lived in one of the tar-paper shacks that clung to the cliff along the edges of the narrow walks.

Inocencia used to help her mother string the washing on lines above the sewage lanes. Her mother washed and washed and washed. Because the neighborhood was dirty and sad, it was all the more necessary to keep things clean and make them gay. José used to try to keep his chicken out of the sewage muck, and Inocencia grew potted plants on the rickety porch which Mr. Ramírez had painted bright green.

A single palm tree grew in the middle of El Fanguito. Inocencia remembers the sound of its swordlike leaves when the evening breeze stirred through them. It was like hands clapping.

Only a few years ago, in El Fanguito, Inocencia heard her parents talk about moving to the housing project where they now live. It wasn't just dream-talk. When El Fanguito was cleared out to make room for a new road and she and José went with their mother and father to the CRUV building to apply for an apartment, they saw a big wall painting there. The painting showed families climbing stairs that led from places like El Fanguito to a housing project like the one where they are now, and then to a house like the one they will soon have. So Inocencia knows that if people work hard, and work together, they can really make their dreams come true. Already she is thinking about a willow tree she wants in the front of the new house.

While all this talk has been going on, the good food has been disappearing fast. Salvadora stops the conversation when she brings dessert to the table. The dessert is one you've never had before — squares of jelly, chewy like gumdrops. It's made from tangy guava fruit which looks something like an apricot. On top of each jelly square is a dab of white cheese, more mellow and crumbly than the kind you usually find in the United States. Felícita offers you half of a fresh lime to squeeze over it. The combination of guava jelly, creamy cheese and lime juice is delicious.

By this time you have become so friendly with the Ramírez family that they invite you to stay with them for the rest of the week which is their vacation time. *"Esta es su casa,"* says Salvadora — "this is your home."

"We'll take you to the coffee plantation where our uncle is boss," promises José. "And to the rain forest," adds Felícita. "Let's go to the Saints' Festival at Loíza Aldea," suggests Inocencia. "We want to go to the Shining Bay," say the twins. "Me, too! Me, too!" echoes Laly. The children want to show you everything.

With so many delightful things to see, how can you say no? Of course you say, "Yes, thank you!" And as Mrs. Ramírez has no extra bed, she arranges for you to spend the night in the apartment of her next-door neighbors. They have a foldaway cot on which you sleep soundly. Children and chickens and dogs wake you early, but you don't mind. You want to be sure not to keep the others waiting.

After breakfast, all ten of you manage to fit yourselves into the Ramírez car. You pass many other cars on the road, equally full. Nobody objects to a little squeezing. It's a holiday. The children, except for little Laly, who is too young for school, know that holidays will soon be over.

A few minutes away from the housing project, you pass the school where the younger children go. It's a long, low concrete building with shutters which are something like Venetian blinds, at the windows. There's no need for glass windowpanes in Puerto Rico's warm climate.

Felícita tells you that school opens the second week in August. Then, in San Juan, the thermometer may show a temperature of up to 100 degrees. The children will want the shutters wide open unless a heavy rain pelts down. It was hot, too, when school closed at the end of May, but Felícita says that the winter months are much cooler, maybe 75 to 85 degrees.

What is school like, you want to know. All the children answer you at once. You discover that in elementary school Salvadora, Felícita, Flavio and Flores have reading and writing, also arithmetic, science, social studies, music and art. All their lessons are in Spanish. They study English from the first grade on. In junior high school, Inocencia has the same subjects, though they are harder. She learns to cook and sew, and boys in her class learn carpentry, electric wiring and other practical skills.

In high school, there's a choice of subjects. José has to take U. S. history and Puerto Rican history, but he has also chosen to take Latin American history and a course called Social and Economic Problems in Puerto Rico. This is because he hopes to work for the government when he grows up. Before he's through high school, he will have had algebra, geometry, solid geometry and trigonometry, two science courses, and maybe French. José goes to a special high school run by the University of Puerto Rico, and Inocencia hopes to pass the exam that will let her go there, too. Students from this school can graduate from the University in three years instead of the usual four.

Inocencia is the president of her school English Club. She is particularly delighted with your visit because it helps her keep the vow she had to make when she joined the club: "I will practice English in every way, in reading, writing and speaking, with teachers and friends."

All the children except José and Inocencia go to double-session schools. Flavio and Flores go from 7:30 to 12:30. Salvadora and Felícita go from 12:30 to 5:30. Mrs. Ramírez explains that there aren't enough schools in San Juan, so the children have to double up that way.

Mrs. Ramírez works in an underwear factory. She makes $1.25 an hour. That's twice as much as she earned when Fomento first brought the factory to Puerto Rico, eleven years ago. She makes extra money if she turns out more than the 90 pairs of underpants she is supposed to finish in a day. She tells you proudly that her name is almost always on the blackboard where the names of the fastest workers of the week are posted.

Mrs. Ramírez wants so many things for the new house she is eager to earn all she can. She finds the work easier now, because the company recently bought new machines. With more machinery, the factory has been able to produce more and Mrs. Ramírez has seen the number of workers double, as well as her wages.

Mr. Ramírez is not sure he's in favor of too many new machines. He's a typesetter at the San Juan *Star,* one of Puerto Rico's most important newspapers. The *Star* is printed in English, and although Mr. Ramírez speaks only Spanish, he has learned how to set the letters of the alphabet to spell English words. Recently the newspaper bought a photographic machine that made typesetting unnecessary. When the huge machine was moved in, all the type-setters were afraid they'd soon have no jobs.

There goes my new house, Mr. Ramírez thought. But the news-paper publisher sent him and some of the other men to school to learn to run the new photographic machine. Mr. Ramírez is learn-ing fast, although he finds it hard. Automation, the use of machines to do jobs which once had to be done by hand, is forcing many Puerto Ricans to learn new skills.

Mr. Ramírez tells you that he wants his children to be well pre-pared to make a good living when they grow up. He's proud that José and Inocencia want to go to the University of Puerto Rico. As you pass the University on the way to the rain forest, he stops the car so that you can all go for a stroll through the beautiful grounds. The buildings are set around a campus shaded with palm trees. The entrances to the buildings are decorated with mosaic tile, in orange, white, blue, beige, and green. Mr. Ramírez tells you that the clay beneath Puerto Rico's soil is just right for making tiles. That's why the island is famous for them.

José points out the building where the Casals Music Festival is held every year. The Festival was started by Pablo Casals, a famous Spanish cello player whose mother was Puerto Rican. José leads you across the campus to the main building and up its pink and blue marble steps. Just inside is a circular lobby, with walls tiled halfway to the ceiling. Wide, rounded arches, such as you will see everywhere in the Caribbean islands, lead out from the lobby. Above them are balconies with mahogany railings. The vertical posts of the railings are smoothly carved in Spanish style.

Students from many countries of North, Central and South America come to the University of Puerto Rico. As a symbol of this, you see the seals of all the American Republics set in a gold circle in the center of the lobby floor. Inside the circle are these words: DEDICATED TO THE AMERICAN REPUBLICS FOR THE ADVANCEMENT OF LEARNING.

As you walk back to the car, José tells you that there's a technical branch of the college at Mayagüez, Puerto Rico's third largest city. One of his cousins studies engineering there.

A few miles beyond the University you are in the countryside, driving between broad fields of sugarcane. You see narrow railroad tracks with small railway cars parked here and there. The cars bring cane from the fields after it is cut at harvest time.

People travel around the island in cars as you are doing. Sometimes they use airplanes to fly from city to city, or they take the bus or a *público*. A público is a privately owned station wagon that leaves when it has enough people to make a good load. Early in the morning, each público owner parks his station wagon in a certain spot. From time to time, he calls out the name of the town where he's going. When his wagon is full, he takes off. Públicos cost less than buses, so people who have more time than money use públicos whenever they can.

At the edge of the road, like a screen between you and the cane fields, you see rows of flamboyant trees in bloom. The trees are so old and so big that they nearly meet above the narrow road. The red blossoms which fall as new ones take their place make it seem as though a red carpet has been spread to take you to the rain forest.

As you approach the forest, the road begins to climb. Felícita, like Inocencia, is especially interested in plants. She explains to you that there are four levels in the rain forest. Each level is named for the type of growth — tree or smaller plant — most common there. The first level, 500 to 1,800 feet above the sea, is named for the wide-branched tabanuco tree. The second level, 1,800 to 2,300

37

feet up, takes its name from the Colorado, a red-trunked, small-leaved tree. Some of the Colorado trees are six to seven hundred years old. One is between 3,000 and 4,000 years old. It's the oldest tree in the Caribbean. The 2,300- to 3,000-foot level is called "Sierra" because there are so many Sierra Palms with starlike blossoms sprouting from the trunks.

At the very top of the forest, 3,000 feet and higher, the plants are called *"el fin."* In English, this means "the end." If you run the two Spanish words together, you get the English word "elfin," very appropriate for the end of the rain forest because all the vegetation at that level is dwarfed by the wind. You will see all these types of growth, except for the el fin, scattered through the three lower levels. You admire them and other beautiful plants as the car climbs up the forest road through the gathering mist.

The abundant moisture — about 250 inches of rain a year — gives the forest its giant growth. Even when the sun is shining, the air is misty. When you stop the car for a few minutes to enjoy the view, the sun and the mist together make you feel as though you were standing in an enormous greenhouse with the sky for a roof. Around you, mountains stretch to the distant sea. Clumps of bamboo trees, tall as a ten-story building, sway in the breeze. Giant tree ferns cling to banks along the roadside, and tall, silvery-leafed secopia trees tower above them.

Banana, grapefruit, orange, wild ginger and mango trees push their way through the lush greenery. The Ramírez twins, Flavio

and Flores spy the ripe mangoes — their favorite fruit — yellow and juicy. How they would love to have some. But they can't pick them. Nobody is allowed to pick anything because the whole rain forest is a national preserve, cared for by the U.S. Forest Service.

Growing high in many of the trees are bromeliads. These are plants with red blossoms and swordlike leaves that thrive on air alone. Here and there African tulip trees burst into crimson bloom. On the ground between the trees grows a little pink flower you may know by the name of "patience." Puerto Ricans call it *im*patience and Felícita shows you why. She picks a seed pod and puts it in the palm of your hand. "Press it ever so gently," she says. You do, and the pod pops wide open, spraying tiny seeds in all directions.

"Look out you don't step on a boa constrictor!" little Laly cries suddenly. Before you have time to panic, Felícita assures you that Laly is only joking. True, there are a few boas in the rain forest, but even the longest ones grow to no more than twelve feet. A boa must be twenty feet long before he can attack.

From where you are, the el fin level of the forest can be reached only by several hours of hiking, so you decide to skip it. Everyone wants to go on to the festival at Loíza Aldea. Felícita assures you that you will see el fin growth in another preserve, the Bosque de Toro Negro. In English it's called the Forest of the Black Bull, and José explains that it's on the way to the coffee plantation where their uncle works.

As you drive toward Loíza Aldea, Inocencia tells you that every Puerto Rican town, city and village has its Saint's celebration. The festival at Loíza Aldea honors Saint James of Santiago, the patron Saint of the village. Each place has a different way of celebrating. In San Juan, people celebrate the festival of the patron Saint, John the Baptist, by dancing in the streets and going for a midnight swim. The swim is supposed to bring good luck for a year.

As Felícita describes other festivals to you, you begin to realize that religion plays an important part in most Puerto Rican holidays. A child's first communion is cause for a family celebration. Last week, when the seven-year-old Ramírez twins received their first communion, the family had a big breakfast afterward. Then they went to visit all their relatives. Each relative gave the twins money. The boys were dressed up in white linen suits for the occasion. Felícita remembers that she wore a long white dress and a veil with a crown on top for her first communion. On Easter Day, too, everybody must wear new clothes if they wish to have good luck.

All the children agree that the most exciting holidays come from Christmas Eve to January 6th. After church services at midnight on Christmas Eve, the family has a special meal of roast pork, boiled bananas, sausages and rice. Outside they may hear a *parranda,* a group of singers, accompanied by a *conjunto* — singing musicians with guitars and dried gourds filled with pebbles which they shake to mark the beat of the music. They are singing *aguinaldos,* the Christmas carols of Puerto Rico. The family will invite the carolers to share their meal.

Next morning, the children find the presents Santa Claus has left. While they open their gifts, they munch *turrón,* a hard candy made with almonds and sugar.

They have hardly become accustomed to their Christmas toys when it's time for the Three Kings to bring still more. On January

5th, the eve of Three Kings' Day, the children pick grass for the camels of the Wise Men, the Three Kings. They fill shoeboxes with the grass and set out glasses of wine for the riders. In the morning, the grass and wine are gone and the presents are there. At noon the family eats heaping plates of *arroz con gandules* and *pasteles*. Arroz con gandules is rice cooked with small white pea-beans, very popular in Puerto Rico. Pasteles is mashed plantain, eggs and pork, rolled in plantain leaves and boiled.

After Three Kings' Day, on February 2nd, comes *Candelaria*. In the morning, people go to church where many candles are burning brightly in memory of the first time the Infant Jesus was taken to the temple by his mother. After the church service, everyone goes out into the countryside to light bonfires to hail the start of the sugarcane harvest.

Inocencia explains that Candelaria, like other Puerto Rican customs, weaves together threads from Puerto Rico's past and present. Spanish, African, Indian and American ways combine in the tapestry of island life. "La Madre Patria" — the mother country, as Mrs. Ramírez calls Spain, "is where our old roots are."

"Yes, but the new ways we earn a living come from the United States," Mr. Ramírez reminds her.

A loud explosion interrupts him. People are throwing firecrackers into the narrow road leading to the village. Ahead of you are crowds of costumed children and grown-ups, and when the bang-bang of the firecrackers dies, you hear the sound of music.

Mr. Ramírez pulls the car under the purple-blossoming jaca-randa trees that line the side of the road. Everybody jumps out and joins the merrymakers. What costumes! Here come three young men in flowing capes covered with gold, red, yellow, turquoise and pink sequins. Bits of mirrors are sewn among the sequins. Their pink trousers and shirts have ruffled cuffs. They wear white gloves and their broad-brimmed, three-cornered hats are piled high with plumes, pompons and artificial flowers. Long streamers flutter from the hats. The masqueraders are pretending to be Spanish conquerors.

Other young men, dressed the same way, ride horseback. The horses move their right legs, fore and hind at the same time, then their left legs, fore and hind, instead of moving the fore right and hind left legs together as most horses do. The ancestors of these *paso fino* — fine-stepping — horses, were brought from Arabia to Spain and from Spain to Puerto Rico. Their gliding gait made them comfortable for sugarcane field overseers who had to spend their days in the saddle.

From Africa came the idea for the masks made of coconut shells worn by devil-dancers with bat-sleeved red costumes. One of them grabs you in his arms and dances you in a circle. "How you feel?" he asks in English, recognizing you as a "Statesider." "Fine," you answer, caught up in the friendly spirit of welcome and gaiety.

He dances you toward a statue of a soldier in a coat of armor, astride a white plaster horse. The soldier is helmeted and bearded and his horse is decked with ribbons and streamers. Horse and rider sit on a flower-covered plank. The rider is Saint James de Santiago, once the patron Saint of the Spanish in long-ago wars, now the Saint of Loíza. Nearby is another smaller statue of Saint James, surrounded by women. The women's statue is supposed to ward off evil spirits. Still a third image, called "Santiaguito," or little Santiago, shows the saint as a young boy. He is the Santiago of the children.

At a given signal, the men, women and children around the three statues pick them up and proceed down the road. Horses and cars follow them, six or seven children on the rear end of each car, snatching a free ride to the next stop, where the firecrackers, music and dancing will begin again. Finally the procession reaches the churchyard and the statues are carried into the church. Outside is a Ferris wheel and a merry-go-round. The fun goes on until late at night — every day for ten days. But there are many people like you who have only one day to spend. The next morning, on the way to the coffee plantation, you pass through other villages holding Saints' festivals. All of you agree that none are so colorful as the festival in Loíza Aldea.

When you leave the last of the villages, the car climbs a winding road through tobacco country. On top of the hills you see barns thatched with palm leaves where the tobacco is stored. Finally you reach the Bosque de Toro Negro. This is the forest with the bent and gnarled dwarf growth which Felícita promised you would stop to see.

It's spooky there in the dusk of the forest. The clouds seem to tear themselves apart on the mountains and fall in tatters across the road. Bearded rams stare at you from the roadside. Through the deepening dark you hear the hoot of an owl, and as you descend, you hear the night music of Puerto Rico — the call of the *coquí*. "Coquí, coquí, coquí," he calls. Another answers, "Coquí — quí — quí — quí — quí!" And suddenly, a choir of coquís greets the new moon.

These tiny frogs are only a little more than an inch long, but you can hear the melody of their song over the hum of all other night creatures. At the coffee plantation, you fall asleep to the concert of the coquís.

This is the plantation where Mr. Ramírez' brother is the *mayordomo,* or foreman, and the next day he shows you around. "Where's the coffee?" you ask, expecting to see the bushes in cleared, neat rows. "Here," says the mayordomo, pointing to thick, woodsy slopes. "The coffee grows under those orange and guaba trees. Coffee needs some sun, but the sunshine must be filtered through much shade, otherwise the coffee berry will be small and flavorless. Coffee also needs rain. That's the reason we plant it high in these hills where the rainfall is heaviest."

"What are those men doing?" you ask, pointing to workers who are digging crescents at the roots of the coffee bushes, on the *up*hill side.

"They are fertilizing the soil," answers the mayordomo. "They put fertilizer at the roots once a year. They are careful to keep the shade trees pruned to let just the right amount of sun come through. You can see the green coffee beans. Here and there along the stalks of the shrubs, you see an occasional reddish one, like this, which is almost ripe."

"When do you pick the coffee beans?" you ask.

"We pick them between the middle of September and the first of January," replies the mayordomo. "We plant new seeds then, too. A coffee bush is good for about twelve years. There must always be young ones coming along to replace the old ones as they die. From February to June the plants bear fragrant white flowers. You should smell the air here then! The hills are full of the fragrance of the coffee blossoms. But harvest time is the gayest time — and the busiest time, too."

"What happens then?"

"Whole families — parents, children and grandparents — come from miles around to pick coffee. The pickers carry baskets strapped to their belts. As fast as they fill their baskets with the ripe berries, they empty them into the family sack. On the steep slopes, sure-footed mules carry the sacks down to the hacienda, or workhouse. If the roads make it possible, the sacks are loaded onto jeeps or trucks instead."

"Where do the pickers come from?" you ask.

"Some of them live in those shacks which we built for them," replied the mayordomo, pointing to shelters scattered from hill to hill. "Others live near enough to go to their own homes at night.

"You can see that there's a lot more to the coffee business than just growing the plants. We have to have houses for the workers, and stables for mules. We have to keep all the machines we use to process the berries in good repair. And we have to make sure we have all the water we need for processing the coffee. We dammed the stream down there for our water supply. The water is pumped up to the hacienda."

"I read in school once that coffee berries were processed by hand," you say doubtfully.

"And so they used to be," the mayordomo answers, "but not often now in these days of automation. Come, you'll see."

The plantation owner, Señor Caballo, and Rafael, one of his sons, are glad to show you the electrically operated machines that sort, clean, take the pulp from the berries and dry the "beans" or seeds which the berries contain. The beans are sent to a coffee cooperative for roasting and selling. Much of the crop will be sold in Europe where fine restaurants and hotels are eager to buy Puerto Rican coffee because they like its rich flavor.

Señor Caballo lives in the city of Ponce, a seaport some 15 miles south of the plantation. He spends about two days a week at his plantation, but he leaves most of the managing to his mayordomo. José went with his uncle once when he had to go to Señor Caballo's home in Ponce to talk business. From José's description you can imagine what a beautiful house it must be. It has two-stories with white-plastered walls and an orange-tiled roof. A high wall protects it from the street in front. The back of the house opens onto a tree-shaded garden. Like most of the finer homes in Puerto Rican cities, Señor Caballo's is on a hill. Straggling up the slope from an inlet of the sea below are the poor shacks like those in El Fanguito, the Ramírez family's old home. This is the way in most Puerto Rican towns and cities — wealth and poverty meet halfway up the hills.

José is glad to see Señor Caballo's son Rafael again. The two start a game of *gallito*. Each boy takes a nut, about the size of a horse chestnut from his pocket. The nuts come from the *algarrobo,* a kind of locust tree. The boys have bored holes in the nuts and looped string through the holes. They wind the string around their fists the way you wind a top. Then each boy slings his nut at the other's. If he hits it and cracks it open, he's the winner.

While José and Rafael are playing, José's uncle, his work done for the day, sits down under a tree and takes out a set of dominoes. Some of the workers see him and gather around. Soon the dominoes are rattling on the cement floor of the patio. The game of dominoes was invented by a Spanish monk named Domine. It's a popular game with the grown-ups. Towns hold domino tournaments, and the winners become popular heroes.

Baseball is popular in Puerto Rico with boys and men of all ages. For small boys, the Little League is a high point of life. José and Rafael both belonged to a Little League when they were younger.

Tomorrow, Rafael is going to La Parguera, a nearby coastal

village where his family has a summer cottage. He invites you to come for an evening sail in the shining bay. Mr. Ramírez says, "Why not? We'll leave early in the morning and stop and show you Ponce. That's our second largest city, after San Juan. You'll see the Saturday market in full swing."

So the next morning you make an early start. In Ponce you go directly to visit the exciting big market before it gets too crowded. The fruits and vegetables look so tempting, you want some of everything you see. Customers jostle each other at the stalls as they try to pick out the reddest tomatoes, the greenest parsley, the plumpest eggplants, the biggest pineapples, the crispest of the curly lettuce heads, the yellowest of the sweet West Indian limes, or the finest of the blue-green squashes which the Ramírez children call "pumpkins."

Mrs. Ramírez heads for one of the stalls selling beans. She figures you will all probably stay at the coffee plantation for a few days, making trips from there into the country, and she wants to put in a supply of food. Beans are a staple Puerto Rican dish. She checks prices at several bean stalls. Then she asks the children: "Which shall it be — the white *gandules,* the pink *haba,* the flavorsome black beans or the meaty red ones?" After checking the children's choice she decides on haba to be cooked with sausage, and red beans to be served in salad. She buys a few scoopfuls of cornmeal, and many scoopfuls of rice, along with two green pep-

pers the size of your thumbnail. Two are all she needs to flavor the rice. These peppers are so hot they will blister your lips if you bite into them raw.

Mr. Ramírez has bought *mabí,* a bark which is used to make a beerlike drink. José has bought some corn kernels for his rooster. They are cheaper here than at home. Mrs. Ramírez has sent the girls to look for the best yams — not sweet potatoes as you might think, but very delicate white yams which are crisp when they are cooked.

Salvadora can't resist adding a breadfruit, which her mother sometimes bakes, sometimes fries as you make French-fried potatoes. The breadfruit tastes something like parsnips.

At another stall in the market, you find goat meat and other meats and fresh fish for sale. Since the pickers' shack where you are staying has no refrigerator, Mrs. Ramírez doesn't buy things which would spoil easily. When you finally leave the crowd and hubbub of the market, everybody carries a string shopping bag loaded with good things to eat.

When you reach the town square or plaza, in the middle of the city, you are startled by a remarkable red, black, blue, green, white and yellow striped building. It looks for all the world like a dizzy circus tent. Then you see fire engines parked inside. This is Ponce's famous old firehouse, the Parque de Bombas. A new and more ordinary firehouse actually serves the city, but the people of Ponce — in Spanish, the Ponceños — love their old one best. Painstakingly, they repaint it every four years. Behind the firehouse and above it rises the pure white dome of a cathedral which stands back to back with the gaudy firehouse.

A double square is around the two buildings. It has a splashing fountain and statues of Puerto Rican heroes. People stop to rest on the shady benches to cool off for a moment as they go about their business in the city's center. Except for its size and its Parque de Bombas, the Ponce plaza is typical of the squares in every Puerto

Rican town. Always the church is there, its bells tolling the hours; always the inviting benches, a statue or two and a bit of welcome shade.

Leaving the square, Mr. Ramírez treats the family to *sangría,* a cooling drink of mild, sweet red wine, sugar, soda water and lime juice. Then you are on your way to La Parguera. Along the road you see oil refineries and chemical plants which Fomento has brought to the island.

Now the road follows the surf-lashed shore, then it winds through country that grows more and more dry. Gone are the brilliant blossoms and the trees with their emerald green foliage. You are driving into southwest Puerto Rico, the island's dry region. Here people make their living by fishing and by taking salt from the inland ponds left by the sea.

La Parguera is an old fishing village. People like Raphael's family are newcomers there. The newcomers have built small white summer homes on piers stretching out into the bay. Attached like garages to the houses are "boat-ports" where they anchor their pleasure boats.

After dark, Rafael takes you and the Ramírez children out in his family's boat. At first, the ride is just a quiet and pleasant evening's sail. Then Rafael turns into an inlet of the bay and a million sparks of greenish light race from the propeller of his motor. The wake behind is a trail of green fire. Fish jump from the water and cascades of sparks fall from their fins. Rafael lowers a bucket over the side. Bringing it up on deck, he tells you to splash the water with your hand. The bucket bubbles with opalescent light. You learn later that the effect is caused by tiny organisms in the water which produce phosphorus. Rafael gives you a small bottle and suggests that you take some of the water home with you. You will be able to see the phosphorescent glow in the dark for as long as the organisms live.

Each trip with the Ramírez family is different. You never know what to expect when you get up in the morning. But you learn through experience that the day will be one to remember.

One morning you set out for San Germán. Next to San Juan, this is the second oldest of the island towns. San Germán is also famous for having the most beautiful of the island's churches, Porta Coeli, meaning "Gate of Heaven." Twenty-four worn brick steps lead up to the church. As they pass through the heavy

wooden doors, the Ramírez children hush their chatter. This is a quiet place so beautiful that even little Laly gazes reverently at the mahogany alter with its blue tiled steps. Mahogany beams support the whitewashed ceiling. In niches along the white walls are the stations of the cross. Each one has small, painted wooden figures with very human faces.

On another day, the twins get their wish to visit the Indian cave on Puerto Rico's north shore, not far from Arecibo. This city is in pineapple and limestone country. Along the way, you pass a range of cone-shaped hills. These are the limestone formations. In the valleys outside the city, you see men and women harvesting pineapple. The women, with broad-brimmed straw hats on their heads to shield them from the sun, cut the fruit with machetes, broad blades almost the length of swords. Men, some with tall baskets on their heads, follow the women. The men work in pairs. One man tosses the pineapple into the other's basket. Then after a while the tosser takes the basket and the carrier tosses. The full baskets are dumped into a truck parked at one end of the field.

Not far from the pineapple fields, the ancient Indian cave is tucked in a limestone hollow. Guarding the hollow is a rocky ledge against which waves beat so fiercely that they have worn a great hole through part of it. Perhaps the cave was washed out by the waves, or perhaps the Indians had to dig it themselves. At any rate, archaeologists say the cave was once a temple and that the carvings on the walls are probably almost 1,500 years old.

Laly and the twins think the carvings are very funny. Some look like faces they might draw themselves. One seems to have a long beard. Others are designs of swirls, spirals and circles. While you are looking at the bearded face in the eerie twilight of the cave something tickles your foot. When you look down, you think you see a small dragon! "No," says Salvadora, reassuringly. "It's only a baby *iguana,* a kind of lizard. And very good eating, too," she adds. "Something like chicken."

The Ramírez children crawl in and you follow them. It is so fascinating that you stay there looking around the vaulted chambers of the cave until Mrs. Ramírez calls you from the top of the steep steps which lead down to it. It's time to get moving! You are almost at the end of your circle round the island. Mr. Ramírez has promised to show you old San Juan.

Old San Juan, except for a few business streets, looks much as it did in Spanish days. The government keeps in that way, for no one wants to forget the beautiful things of Puerto Rico's past. The houses have big shutters and mahogany-railed balconies. The narrow streets — really only alleys — are paved with cobblestones of blue slag — leftover material from iron foundries in Spain. Some sidewalks are so narrow that you have to walk single file.

Early in the morning, Mr. Ramírez takes all of you to El Morro, a fort atop a sandstone bluff at the western tip of San Juan. El Morro means "the bluff" and truly, it's hard to tell where the fort stops and the natural stone, on which it is built, begins. The surf has battered the stone at the base so that fort and rock seem to belong together, all of one piece.

You enter El Morro through one of Puerto Rico's many U. S. military bases. In the courtyard of the fort you meet a U. S. National Park Service guide who takes you around the ramparts. He has a little trouble with the Ramírez twins. They keep trying to

climb into the lookouts where Spanish guards once watched for enemy ships. They like to slide down the chute along which soldiers rolled cannons into firing position.

After the guide has discouraged the twins from these adventures, he explains that it took 247 years to build El Morro. When you run your hands over the 40-foot-thick walls, you can understand why.

From the lower courtyard, the guide points out giant walls that curve in and out along the seafront, where to the east, you see another fort, San Cristóbal. Between the two forts is a slum. "It looks very much like El Fanguito where we used to live," says José.

As Mr. and Mrs. Ramírez stand there high above the ugly slum, they are thinking about their past life in El Fanguito and about the good things they see in the future — for themselves and for Puerto Rico. Mr. Ramírez says he'd like to see the island become part of the

United States as the fifty-first state in the Union. Mrs. Ramírez thinks it better for Puerto Rico to remain a commonwealth, but she would like to see closer ties with continental U. S. A. She would particularly like to vote for the President.

José tells you that his uncle belongs to the Independence Party. This is a small political party which wants Puerto Rico to become a free country, completely independent from the U. S. A. He has learned in school that in 1966 a commission created by the U. S. Congress and the Puerto Rican Legislative Assembly agreed that there ought to be a plebiscite, an island-wide vote to give all Puerto Ricans a chance to say what they think. Should the island become a state, remain a commonwealth with some changes, or gain its independence? Mr. Ramírez hopes that such a plebiscite will be held soon.

Before Operation Bootstrap began to succeed, about 45,000 Puerto Ricans a year moved to the United States and about a million of them have stayed. Most of them live in New York City. The rest are scattered throughout our fifty states. They left the island in the hope of earning more money and making a better living for themselves than they could at home.

Now that Puerto Rico is becoming more prosperous, people can look forward to making a better living there at home. Not so many of them want to leave now. It's easy for you to understand why. During the time you've spent with the Ramírez family, you've learned to love their beautiful island.

Today the Ramírez family wouldn't dream of moving to the mainland to stay, although they'd all like to come to visit. José's uncle told you that his two oldest children live in New York. Two younger ones went a few years ago, but they have recently moved back home. They are part of the turning tide — more Puerto Ricans are coming home these days than leaving.

What fun it will be, you think, when your visit is over, to correspond with your Puerto Rican friends. But the Ramírez children think it would be more fun for you to come visit them again — and soon.

As you stand there on the ramparts of El Morro, Felícita bends over and picks, from the grass between the stones, a little yellow flower that looks like a primrose. "It's the wild margarita," she says, "the flower of San Juan. Keep it to remember us by."

## SAY IT IN SPANISH*

| English | Spanish | Pronunciation |
|---------|---------|---------------|
| Hello | Hola | *Oh*-lah |
| | Que tal (formal) | *Kay*-tahl |
| Goodbye | Adiós | *Ah*-dee-*oh* |
| Please | Por favor | Por-r fay-*vor-r* |
| Thank you | Muchas gracias | *Moo*-chah *Grah*-tzee-ah |
| We are friends | Somos amigos | *Soh*-mohs ah-*mee*-gohs |

* Most Puerto Ricans, and some people in Central America and South America do not pronounce the *s* in *adios* and *muchas gracias*. In Spain, the *s* is sounded.

# HOW TO PRONOUNCE FOREIGN WORDS IN THIS BOOK*

| Word | Pronunciation | Word | Pronunciation |
|---|---|---|---|
| aguinaldos | ah-gee-*nahl*-dohs | La Borinqueña | Lah Boh-reen-*key*-nyah |
| algarrobo | ahl-gah-*roh*-boh | | |
| Arecibo | Ah-ray-*see*-boh | Laly | *Lah*-lee |
| arroz con gandules | ah-*rohs* cone gahn-*doo*-leys | La Parguera | La Par-*gair*-ah |
| | | L'Escuela | Les-*kwail*-ah |
| arroz con pollo | ah-*rohs* cone poy-oh | Loíza Aldea | Loh-*eez*-ah Ahl-*day*-ah |
| Caballo | Kah-*bah*-loh | Luis Muñoz Rivera | *Loo*-ees *Moon*-yohs Ree-*vair*-ah |
| Camión de bomberos | kah-me-*on* day bom-*bey*-rohs | | |
| conjunto | kohn-*hoon*-toh | mabí | mah-*bee* |
| coquí | koh-*kee* | marguarita | mar-gah-*reet*-ah |
| Corporación de Renovación Urbana y Vivienda | Cor-poh-rah-*thyon* day rey-noh-vah-*thyon* Oor-*bah*-nah e Vee-*vyen*-dah | Marín | Mah-*reen* |
| | | Mayagüez | Mah-*yah*-gways |
| | | mayordomo | *my*-hyor-*doh*-moh |
| | | Pablo Casals | *Pah*-bloh Kah-*sahls* |
| El Fanguito | Ell Fahn-*gee*-toh | parranda | pah-*rahn*-dah |
| el fin | el *feen* | pasteles | past-*ey*-leys |
| El Morro | Ell *Mor*-oh | Ponce | *Pon*-say |
| Esta es su casa | *Es*-tah es soo *cah*-sah | Ponce de León | *Pon*-say day Lay-*ohn* |
| | | público | *pooh*-blee-koh |
| Felícita | Fey-*lee*-see-tah | Rafael | *Rah*-fah-ell |
| Flavio | *Flah*-vee-oh | | |
| Flores | *Floor*-eys | Salvadora | Sahl-vah-*doh*-rah |
| | | San Cristóbal | Sahn Krist-*oh*-bahl |
| gallito | gah-*yee*-toh | San Germán | Sahn Hair-*mahn* |
| | | sangría | sahn-*gree*-ah |
| haba | *hah*-bah | San Juan Bautista | Sahn *Hwahn* Bow-*teest*-ah |
| hacienda | hah-*thyen*-dah | | |
| | | Santiago | Sahn-tee-*ah*-goh |
| | | Señor | *Seh*-nhyor |
| independendista | in-day-pen-den-*tee*-stah | Serenidad | Say-reh-nee-*dahd* |
| Inocencia | Inoh-*cen*-see-ah | Tabonuco | Tah-boh-*noo*-koh |
| | | toro | toh-roh |
| jíbaro | *he*-bar-oh | turrón | tour-*rohn* |
| José Ramírez de Rosas | Hoh-*say* Rah-*me*-reys dey *roh*-sahs | usufruct | use-*oo*-frookt |

*Italics indicate stress.

# HISTORY

Pre-Columbian times — Island inhabited by Indians; oldest tribe the Tainos, later Arawaks and invading Caribs.

1493 — Columbus discovers Puerto Rico.

1508 — Spanish colony established near San Juan, with Ponce de León as first governor.

1528-1576 — French attacks on Puerto Rico.

1595-1598 — British attacks led by Sir Francis Drake and the Earl of Cumberland.

1624 — Dutch attack the island.

1600-1800 — Puerto Rico becomes a haven for smugglers and pirates from all Europe.

1797 — Renewed British effort to capture Puerto Rico.

1815 — Trade with Puerto Rico opened to the world.

1897 — Spain signs a charter promising Puerto Rico home rule.

1898-1900 — Spanish-American War. Defeated, Spain cedes Puerto Rico to the U. S. A. American military rule of the island.

1900 — Civilian rule (by the U.S.) established by the Foraker Act, passed in U.S. Congress.

1917 — Jones Act passed in U.S. Congress gives Puerto Ricans American citizenship and power to elect both houses of their legislature.

1940 — Muñoz Marín founds Popular Democratic Party and starts Operation Bootstrap.

1947 — Jones Act amended to permit Puerto Ricans to elect their own governor, judges, cabinet members.

1949 — Muñoz Marín becomes first elected governor.

1964 — Muñoz Marín refuses to run for governor any longer. Roberto Sanchez Vilella, of the Popular Democratic Party, is elected. A commission to examine the status of Puerto Rico, with particular reference to the United States, is jointly established by the U.S. Congress and the Puerto Rican legislature.

1966 — The Status Commission reports, calling for a plebiscite in which Puerto Ricans can express their preference among the following alternatives for the future: statehood, liberalized Commonwealth, independence.

# Index

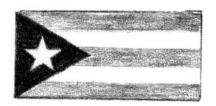